Even When Life Doesn't Play Nice

One Child's Journey from Unfavorable Beginnings

- A Memoir -

PATRICIA CHRISTIAN PUNCHES

CROSSBOOKS
PUBLISHING

CrossBooks™
A Division of LifeWay
1663 Liberty Drive
Bloomington, IN 47403
www.crossbooks.com
Phone: 1-866-879-0502

First published by CrossBooks 9/7/2010

ISBN: 978-1-6150-7300-9 (sc)
ISBN: 978-1-6150-7301-6 (hc)

Library of Congress Control Number: 2010911543

Cover art by Patricia Punches

Printed in the United States of America

This book is printed on acid-free paper.

To all my extended family and friends throughout the years, thank you for the priceless and cherished memories.

To my beloved husband, children, and grandchildren, who have fulfilled my greatest dreams, you are life's joy and inspiration.

To Jesus Christ, my Lord and Savior, all praise, honor, and glory to You forever and ever.

Dad, Mom, and Bill ... I love you.

Contents

- Acknowledgments -

I extend heartfelt gratitude to my husband, Dennis, for his offerings of encouragement, technical support, and soundboard reviews throughout the writing of this memoir ... and to the outstanding team at CrossBooks for believing in my work and so wonderfully producing it.

- Introduction -

It was a typical evening at our home—my husband working on a repair in the garage while I completed a few tasks on the inside. As I reached over to turn off the den light, an overpowering, but wonderful force suddenly enveloped me. I had experienced God's presence before, but this was of an unprecedented magnitude. There was an electricity of expectancy and excitement that I had never previously felt. Then, as if the stage had been set, the second remarkable occurrence took place—not in audible words but in a crystal clear message sent straight to my innermost being, I instantly knew I was to write a book … one about my childhood. Understandably, I was somewhat bewildered, but in an ecstatic kind of way as the presence remained ever strong. I now knew God was speaking to me, and in the spiritual realm I had never experienced anything so direct and specific as this. As I was mentally processing these happenings, I thought of my list of "to dos" and how writing a book, much less an autobiography, was not even a blip on the radar! I had always enjoyed writing and communicating, having composed a few smaller projects, but certainly had never authored a book or even aspired to do so.

The Holy Spirit continued to affirm what had taken place, and as my husband entered the house I intercepted him, attempting to articulate this divine encounter. Cognizant of my somewhat unusual childhood and God's constant protection over me, we realized simultaneously that He had a purpose in this, with my responsibility being to follow His lead. I had such a burning desire to begin immediately that I embarked upon my "assignment" that very evening, barely stopping until I had penned the last word. At the onset, I felt waves of apprehension and inadequacy for such a task, but as I discussed the matter with God, He continually reminded me this was of Him, and His provision was mine every step of the way. As I continued in faith, I was fervently determined to complete what the Lord had called me to do … for whatever plans He had therein. It developed into a truly incredible experience, and as I instated the final period, it was exactly one month from the day I started to the day I finished. With some further expansion and final editing over the months to follow, my mission became complete. The pages you are about to read are the result of my testimony.

Chapter One

FUN WITH DICK AND JANE

Looking back, 1950 seems like it was an especially good year to be born. World War II had ended, bringing renewed hope and optimism to the now-flourishing suburban America. Affluence was surging as the workforce offered husbands greater opportunities than ever and "modern" housewives enjoyed unprecedented comforts in the home. My parents, Ray and Doris Christian, were two such people who found themselves in the midst of this new golden era. Living in suburbia, they enjoyed a comfortable bedroom community just outside of Milwaukee. By the year 1949, their beautiful five-year-old little boy, Charles William, was on his way to becoming a proud big brother.

In December, due to employment opportunities as well as a desire to leave the excessively cold and snowy Wisconsin winters, the three moved south to the mid-state city of Decatur, Illinois. It was there, on June 8, 1950, that I, Patricia Ann Christian, was born into the family. Because of time constraints, a very small and modest home had been purchased, with the intention of relocating to a more spacious residence in the near future. I, in fact, was born at home in this recently acquired two-bedroom bungalow. Tragically, and soon after, however, our mother was overtaken by illness, leaving Bill, who was six, and me, five months, motherless. To say my father was in great despair over the loss of his beloved wife would be a grave understatement, and now with two small children for whom to care, he had a monumental challenge and responsibility before him. And so I never knew my mother on a personal level, but later came into the knowledge of what a truly beautiful, gracious, and talented woman she was.

Because of the huge void left by my mother's absence, my great-Aunt Icie came to stay with us, and in caring for Bill and me, she provided our dad with some much needed support. I loved Aunt Icie, and even though I was very young, as she remained with us only until I was three, I retain some especially fond memories of what a nurturing and doting mother figure she was. Her successor was Mildred, who came onboard after responding to my dad's advertisement for help with housekeeping and childcare. Mildred was a kind, loving woman to whom I became very attached and vice-versa, until about two years later when she was called away for personal reasons. It was a teary goodbye when she was seated in the train at the Decatur depot, waving to me through the window and departing for St. Louis. I would really miss Mildred.

Eva came to live with us next, and although she was somewhat stern and distant, she seemed to take her duties seriously in caring for us and tending to the house. One day, however, a neighboring boy "upset the apple cart" when he peered into the bedroom window where she was dressing. From what I remember at six years old, she became very angry and even more so with Dad for not sharing in her level of antagonism. As a result, she promptly departed in a huff!

At this point, things took a downward turn as my dad unsuccessfully sought capable live-in replacements to care for my brother, me, and our home. A succession of not so caring, unqualified women became our misfortune, and one by one my father would dismiss them as they revealed in a variety of ways their disinterest and incompetence. I don't recall who had been hired at this juncture, but one morning in second grade I awakened with no one home, so dressed for school and proceeded to the neighbors' where I always met with Giggy, one of my favorite playmates, and we would walk to school together. His mother, Mrs. Lehman, upon answering the door, said, "Patty, it's ten o'clock and school has long been in session." As I must have looked confused and frightened, she empathetically assured me it would be okay and proceeded to pin a note on my dress for the teacher to read. Not long after, when again awakening alone, I proceeded to prepare for school but found there was nothing left in my closet to wear. I called Dad at work and he then came home, attempting to iron a dress he had found in a laundry bag. I still recall his gallant efforts as he bent over the ironing board trying to press a little dress with row after row of ruffles. I believe the dress became seriously scorched and the "housekeeper" seriously fired! It was most unfortunate, as it seemed the intended party had often only been present when it was time to receive a paycheck.

Then there was Maxine, a divorcee who brought with her a rather unruly two-year-old. She, too, proved to be disinterested in her duties, offering little toward cooking, cleaning, or childcare. One day while out playing, I decided to collect some dandelions, of which we had a plentiful supply, and present them to Maxine as a gift. I stepped onto the porch and attempted to open the door, but for some reason it was locked which seemed most unusual. Standing on the threshold and tiptoes, I peered through the square glass window, recognizing her ex whom I had previously met. As they were embraced on the floor I was completely puzzled in my innocence. Stepping down and laying my crumpled bouquet on the milk box, I turned to look for my friends. Later conveying the incident to Dad, all I knew, after that, was I never saw Maxine again.

The milk box brings back some special memories. When I was very young products were delivered from the local dairies by horse-drawn wagons. Several of the old city streets were brick, and I still recall the sound of the horse's hooves clippity-clopping over them as they traveled from house to house. Many homes had the silver insulated box on the porch next to the door, where order requests were left to then be fulfilled by the driver. Even after the advent of trucks, this routine continued until home delivery became obsolete with the newly evolving supermarket.

After Maxine came a rather large woman whose name I don't remember, but who sent me to the corner grocery for ice cream and snacks while she watched the afternoon soap operas. She, as well, provided very little care, and the house continued in a state of neglect. Consequently, this made her stay also a brief one. Over the two and a half years following Mildred's departure, and in spite of Dad's ongoing efforts, I would witness the end of Eva and an insalubrious succession of "caretakers."

Undoubtedly, the resulting negligence had potential for emotional harm, but overall I was a happy child, seeming to draw from a well within, a place beyond myself. Probably the neighborhood ragamuffin, I was usually quite cheerful, playing the days away with the outdoor gang. Albeit, we had a "less than perfect" household, but there was an ongoing sense of Dad's presence, as he was ever adoring and I was always assured of his love. It was an era when men were commonly reserved about showing emotion and outward affection. Still, Dad had his ways of making the connection, for after a meal he would leave his chair, affectionately stopping by mine to tickle my side or gently tug at my hair while on his way to the living room. In my youngest years, I recall running to the door as I heard Dad arrive and park out front. As he came up the walk I would run to meet him, all to be rewarded with a toss in the air and an ultra-smooth landing. That was the anticipated greeting of the day until somewhere in my sixth year when Dad gently informed me, "Susie (childhood nickname), I think you're getting too big for this maneuver!"

Between efforts of securing household assistance, Bill would be appointed to stay home in evenings with me while Dad returned to the shop. I remember, later on, we had some parakeets, and at times we let them out of their cages to fly freely around the living room. Not conducive to a sanitary environment, this only added to the already "unkempt" state of affairs. In fact, cleanliness became such an issue that the height of my fears was realized when our home became overridden with bugs. I was afraid to get up at night, wanting to avoid stepping on the floor, and turning on a lamp was an especially scary scene! One evening, after returning from a drive-in movie and parking the car in the garage, we walked up the sidewalk and entered the house from the back. When Dad switched on the light I couldn't help but scream, for I was horrified by the sight of roaches overtaking our kitchen, and now running in all directions like rats off a sinking ship! Dad, out of disdain rather than fear, emphatically instructed, *"Quiet down and start stompin'!"* I truly do not know how I rested at night during that period of time, given the mental images, but apparently sleep takes over even in a wary circumstance. To this day, I'm convinced the frightening "reign of roaches" significantly contributed to my well-earned title of "clean freak!"

I remember getting our first television when I was between four and five years old. A black-and-white with rounded screen and wooden cabinet, it sat on the floor at one end of the living room. This was a huge development in the arena of home entertainment, as people had "watched" only their radios prior. My earliest memory of TV was the premier children's show, *Captain Kangaroo,* who, along with his sidekick, Mr. Green Jeans, became a household name. Later, during my grade school years, Saturday morning cartoons and *Sky King* became an anticipated time of the week. Together we watched some favorite sitcoms and Dad enjoyed the popular drama, *Gunsmoke.* Of course he always watched the evening news and it was understood this was to be uninterrupted, barring an emergency!

I so loved and respected Dad all the years of my life, and as I was growing up, knew he was the smartest man in the whole world. On several occasions, I told him he should be president of the United States. Although he had no aspirations along those lines, he did possess a great deal of political savvy and was well-respected for being a kind, honorable, and generous man; generous, but not frivolous. Dad, like many others, had endured the Great Depression of 1929, which continued through the following decade. The few times he mentioned the subject, apparent were the devastating effects and aftermath of trauma. My grandparents had barely managed to retain their home and farm while countless other families went into foreclosure and lost everything. It was, indeed, a traumatic time, and I sensed Dad's remaining apprehensions and precautionary efforts should, heaven forbid, history repeat. It seemed those who had lived through this demoralizing experience were very in tune with hard work, a good measure of frugality, and maintaining substantial reserves. Since moving to Decatur, Dad had established a thriving machine shop business and later he invented a product which evolved into a corporation with an international clientele. For more than being an intelligent, industrious entrepreneur, I deeply respected him as an utmost honest and caring man. Giving priority to customer needs, he believed that in providing a quality product and excellent service, a successful and rewarding career would result. With this policy at the forefront, his efforts produced a flourishing business over the many ensuing years.

My dad's noble character had a great impact, and I grew up knowing that honesty and integrity were of the highest priorities. With the responsibilities of his business, my father most often returned to work until late in the evening. Knowing those first years after losing our mother were particularly difficult, undoubtedly the consuming demands and resulting successes of his corporate duties were very therapeutic. My heart still goes out to my brother, as being only six years old when our mother was taken, he was at an especially vulnerable age to lose his closest bond. During a time when misfortunes were often not discussed, there was very little healthy awareness of how to deal with such things, regarding counseling and outside assistance. As a result, Bill was somewhat withdrawn and non-conversational. A quiet, gentle soul, he also became an absolute genius in the arena of machinery or anything mechanical. As the years continued, he and my dad were an outstanding team of creativity in the workplace, and Bill thrived in this environment, which was the perfect channel through which his talents could flow.

As for me, I loved school and learning, playing outside with friends, and being a happy, optimistic little urchin! If I was to display the predicted effects of having been neglected maternally and living in an unstable household, no one told me, so I just went on being happy and enjoying my life as I knew it. Not that I was without insecurities, as it was certain they were there, but my love for life, adventure, and those around me seemed to rise above the negatives, holding any hindering forces and self-doubts at bay. Many summer days were enjoyed to the fullest, as kids from the "hood," Cindy, Greg (Giggy), Cheryl, Linda, and I would run from dawn 'til dusk playing "cowboys and indians," tag, and hide-and-seek. Usually around twilight Dad would call, "Susie, time to come home!" There was something magical about those childhood summers that seemed to last forever, and when a custard cone from the corner grocery was a very special treat. The 1950s were a decade of simplicity and a time of much greater innocence.

When school would resume after Labor Day, one of the year's highlights was the Riverside Fall Festival. An annual fundraiser, the grounds were filled with neighbors, food, games, and laughter, and we kids enjoyed every moment of the fun and festivities. Our home was located just next to the grade school, so it was an especially special part of my childhood, given I had benefit of the playground at almost any time.

Mrs. Brown was my first-grade teacher, and I absolutely loved everything about school: learning, social interaction, classroom community, and the whole structure of our days. I was always eager to please and excited about learning anything new. *Fun with Dick and Jane* was our reader, and I still have my original book. I was enchanted by the stories, the pictures, and the whole concept of being able to read the words myself. Dick, Jane, Sally, Mother, Father, Grandmother, Grandfather, Spot, and Puff became beloved characters and friends, and I was endeared by the portrait of such a happy, loving, *complete* family. I recognized the interaction and wholesome relationships as being most commendable. I also enjoyed the simple but delightful storylines of fun and adventure. On the play front our neighborhood *was* Dick, Jane, Sally, and friends, for we, too, enjoyed those same close, happy relationships with endless days of fun. And the positive image the book presented of home and family life especially became imprinted on my mind, for I knew it was something very good and well worth aspiring toward.

- Chapter Two -

Love Came Down

In second grade I had a teacher of whom I was very fond. Miss Casey was an attractive young woman, newly out of college and just beginning her career in education. She developed a special affection for me, and I became what was termed "teacher's pet." Most likely she had been briefed on my general background and situation at home, resulting in an outreach of compassion. This relationship reinforced my love for school, and I always brought home good report cards. One Saturday Miss Casey invited me to her apartment, not far from my home, to bake cookies and spend time together. Her genuine kindness was a real stroke on the positive side and I absorbed the love like a sponge, skipping home that day with a gift and cookies in hand.

It was 1957, and at seven years old I was now eligible and eager to become a Brownie. This proved to be an enjoyable and rewarding endeavor, given the camaraderie, activities, and responsibilities involved. Donned in my official uniform, complete with beanie, I was on the noble mission one particular day of selling Girl Scout cookies in my neighborhood. With my cardboard carrier well stocked I tenaciously stayed at the task, walking from house to house until my case was empty and money complete. I relished the challenge as well as the sense of accomplishment and continued to enjoy, over the course of a year, my entire Brownie experience.

On Tuesdays after school there was an independent and open invitation to attend Good News Club. I, along with several other classmates, would walk to the house on the corner diagonally across the street. Mrs. Leonard welcomed us at the side door, ushering us down a flight of stairs and into her basement. Here, rows of folding chairs faced the front where there was a large flannelgraph—a flannel-covered board on a tri-pod and with figures used for storytelling. There was also a curtain beyond that separating the "classroom" from the utility area. I thrived on Mrs. Leonard's teachings as she told us of God's love and stories from the Bible, illustrating them with the wonderful figures placed on the flannelgraph. She was a kind, grandmotherly type, firm in her faith and with a heart for children. One particular Tuesday, after learning about the special love Jesus had for children, Mrs. Leonard asked us to all bow our heads in prayer. Following, with heads still bowed, she asked if anyone would like to receive Jesus into his or her heart and come to know Him in a deep and personal way. If so, we were asked to raise our hand. Clearly, there was a tugging at my heart, and in that moment I raised my hand, not knowing that would be the single most important decision I would ever make. After a short pause, giving opportunity for others to respond, Mrs. Leonard then invited me behind the curtain, dismissing the other children. It was an exceptionally meaningful and precious time as I repeated after her in prayer, receiving Jesus as my personal Lord and Savior. I took seriously every word that was spoken, confident that Jesus was my very best friend and loved me more than I could ever know. I left Good News Club that afternoon fully aware something special had taken place, but I could not begin to know at the time just how truly special it was. For her many faithful years of devotion to children, Mrs. Leonard now enjoys her reward in heaven.

On the home front, the troubling situation with household help continued, for in spite of Dad's efforts we were still sorely lacking in a responsible housekeeper and caregiver. One evening, the individual currently on duty had somewhere she wanted to go, and it seemed I was the only glitch in her plans. Bill was with Dad at the shop while she, theoretically, was caring for me at home. I did not know to where we drove, but once arrived she put me to bed in a small, dingy house, instructing me to sleep until her return. Alone in this strange, foreboding place, I felt frightened, but then remembered Mrs. Leonard and all she had taught me about God's love. Moreover, He was now living in my heart, caring for and watching over me. I closed my eyes, praying that Jesus be near, and in that moment a very real comfort and security was present, as I then drifted into a deep sleep.

When I was seven going on eight I could no longer read the chalkboard at school with clarity, so Dad took me for an eye exam which revealed my need for glasses. The doctor also advised that I have adequate light for reading, so we left his office and proceeded to Woolworth's where we selected a wall-mounted lamp to place over the side of my bed. Woolworth's was a popular "five and dime," or dime store, as it was called during the 1950s, and it offered an assortment of household items. Also available were small pets. It was always exciting to walk through the far corner of the building where bright orange fish swam in aquariums, bowls held tiny turtles paddling in shallow water, and a community of blue, green, and yellow parakeets chirped noisily in their cages. This was most likely where our birds had been purchased, and Bill and I enjoyed them immensely.

During those times when I was home alone, I learned to fend for myself and prepare for what arose. One summer day I was to attend a friend's birthday party. I had a present but no paper with which to wrap it. As a seven-year-old it must have seemed like Kleenex would be a satisfactory substitute, for that is what I used, securing the tissue with tape. I was sad and embarrassed when the children made fun of my attempts and the not-so-beautiful offering. There were probably similar reactions over my sometimes less-than-perfect appearance, given I had no motherly guidance and my clothes were not always well matched. I admired the girls who wore such beautiful dresses and had numerous can-cans to make them stand out full. And their shiny patent-leather shoes were the perfect finishing touch. But these moments of admiration were fleeting, for I was busy enjoying life and happy to be living my own.

There was also that day in the school year when it was time for parent visitation, and most often it was the mother who attended. I envied the children whose mothers would arrive so neatly dressed and smiling, as they graciously and quietly slipped to the back of the room to be seated. It was one of those times when I especially missed having a mother of mine, one who would enter the room the same causing me to well up with pride. I realized my classmates were very lucky … probably much more than did they. There were also the treats a mother would bring when it was her son or daughter's birthday. On these occasions we all enjoyed a special cookie or cupcake along with our daily milk. This issue was easier, since I had a birthday in June when school was not in session.

Then, one most memorable day something quite wonderful happened that would completely change my world. In Dad's ongoing quest to recruit good household assistance, a woman by the name of Mae answered his ad, and after meeting she was hired as our newest, and happily last, live-in housekeeper. Mae was sixty-four years old when she arrived, and I had just recently turned eight. Born in 1894, she was an old-world, hardworking pioneer type who, along with her brothers, had been raised on a farm and was capable of mastering most any task. She had experienced a difficult life, having already lost two husbands and sons, which left her with one son living. To support herself she had taken employment by keeping house for others and working as a cook in local cafes. The timing was right, as she was between jobs and saw my father's advertisement in the paper. It was very fortunate that Mae was of such strong fortitude, for the picture of our home when she first arrived would surely have scared most anyone else away. By this point, household duties had been so long-neglected that a feminine touch was in desperate need. Thankfully, she saw past the present disaster and looked forward to the possibilities.

A major breakthrough occurred that day, and I soon felt a wonderful comfort and security. Mae dug into the enormous task at hand, cleaning, exterminating, and with Dad's assistance, painting and tiling. Our house was beginning to feel like a home and a place of peace and refuge. She prepared three meals a day, making certain we were all well nourished, and everything tasted exceptionally good. Things had changed considerably from my days of not so long ago, when all alone I would search the refrigerator or pantry for something to eat. The transformation Mae brought was remarkable, and that she was willing to rise to such a monumental task, even more remarkable. For her extreme willingness, I would be eternally grateful. The house was now clean but still very modest. After losing his wife, Dad never did move us to a more spacious home. It seemed he had lost interest in that aspect of things, so I grew up in the same small house in which I was born, not really departing until the day I married.

Mae initiated the replacement of many household items, from furniture to draperies to bedspreads to linens, and there was now laundry on the backyard clothesline just as there was at the other homes. Upon her arrival I had one remaining dress, as a previous "party" had taken my others. We therefore enjoyed our first trip to town in order to secure some much-needed clothing. Although she kept me very well groomed, there was little emphasis on style or glamour. As a result, a few of those grade school photos were humbling, revealing some very unflattering hair days! Mae also had quite the green thumb, for not only was there dramatic change to the inside, but amazing things equally transformed on the outside. Soon our front and back yards were ablaze with colorful flowers, including roses, peonies, tulips, pansies, and morning glories. She even planted a garden from which we enjoyed a bountiful harvest. This included pumpkins, and the fried blossoms became a family favorite. Soon after, there was a grape arbor added, and later an apple tree. I loved how my dad began to enjoy a stroll every morning after breakfast. He would observe the flowers, the fruits, and the garden, as well as the squirrels chasing one another through the trees. Our house had finally become a home, and it was incredibly wonderful.

While Dad and Bill were at the shop on weekends, Mae and I rode the bus to town on Saturdays, even if just to window shop, but always for an ice cream treat at Woolworth's soda fountain. I was so thankful for Mae, our mutual love, and her ever-consistent presence. She later noted that wherever we went during those early days, I always held tightly onto her hand, making certain we were never separated.

Some most remarkable and significant events had taken place over these past several months, as if a positive force had intervened. In my heart, I knew *Someone* wonderfully divine was reaching down .... And I was reaching back.

- Chapter Three -

THE OLD TIN GOOSE

My dad was a self-made pilot in the late 1940s. Owning his own plane, a four-passenger red Stinson, he affectionately named it "The Old Tin Goose." From my earliest memories, we almost always made long-distance trips by flight and these were typically to northern Indiana, where all our relatives on Dad's side of the family lived. Highly anticipating these visits, we would be warmly welcomed and treated like royalty. I loved being with my grandma, grandpa, aunts, uncles, and cousins and intuitively knew from the youngest age just how precious these times were, for we were family and there was a very special and loving bond. While in flight I could barely wait to get to Grandma and Grandpa's house, where everyone would meet in those early days and we cousins were thrilled to reunite. Sadly, Grandma passed away when I had just turned six, so I never had a chance to really know her. I do remember, however, how kind and gentle she was and that she always sat on a daybed in the living room due to a severe condition of arthritis. Grandpa devotedly and lovingly cared for her during those years of incapacitation, and their relationship was a testament of true love and commitment, as well as a cherished legacy for the entire family.

After Grandma's passing, Dad planned a vacation to Florida wherein Grandpa would accompany us. Understanding the incredible loss he was experiencing, Dad, in his compassion, felt this would help ease the grief and provide some encouragement. This was not a trip for the Old

Tin Goose because Dad had been unsuccessful in getting Grandpa inside the plane. Everyone else in the family had been up for a spin, but he just did not trust these "newfangled flying machines." Finally, on one particular visit Dad negotiated a deal, promising if he would take a seat on the passenger side, they would merely taxi down the tarmac for refueling. Confident the plane would not be airborne, Grandpa finally got his ride, the wheels never leaving the ground! Incidentally, the Florida road trip in our green, '50 Chrysler proved to be a great success and a real source of enjoyment.

My dad came from a farming family, and all our relatives remained in that tradition. They raised either corn and soybeans or livestock or both. My father, being an adventurous, independent type, was the sole member who blazed a completely different trail, leaving the farm for the "big city." His mechanical talents provided him employment in the machinery industry, and he became a successful salesman for a very large firm. This gave opportunity for him and my mother to travel and live in several large cities across the East during their early years of marriage. Returning to visit family caused quite a flurry of excitement, as Ray and Doris always brought with them a wealth of stories and gifts from their travels. This, of course, was relayed to me by aunts and cousins, all who dearly loved and well-remembered my parents' returns.

Our visits with family in Indiana were a joy untold, and for a city kid like me, it was icing on the cake spending time on the farm. All of us cousins would be utterly ecstatic, exploring the barn, climbing the hay mow, and perusing the farmyard with the various animals. We ran and played like there was no tomorrow, for there was nothing more exhilarating than the adventures we shared!

Now that Mae was part of our family, she made several trips along with us, soon becoming a full-fledged member of the clan. I never wanted to leave at the end of our visits, but once Dad rounded us up, all the family by way of a convoy would accompany us to the airstrip. After hugs and goodbyes we boarded the plane, Dad check-listing the engine and controls. As everyone stood alongside, anticipating the grand finale, he positioned the plane down the runway and then gave full throttle. As we lifted off, gaining enough distance and altitude to loop around, we then banked steeply, the side of the plane sloped toward the ground. We were now face to face, family below looking up and waving while we looked down and were waving back. Holding on to the moment, we all too quickly lost sight and were soon cruising through the sky toward home.

One of our longer flights was to Colorado Springs where Mae's brother and family lived. They had graciously invited us to visit for a weekend, and it proved to be a wonderful time. Clarence and Ruth treated us to a generous measure of hospitality, including great conversation and wonderful meals. They also had three college-age daughters who were remarkably attentive and kind—quite an exceptional treat for a mere nine-year-old. Our flight approach had not been quite so smooth, as we arrived to some rather inclement weather. There was a thunderstorm in progress, which required us to circle Pike's Peak until receiving clearance for landing. During this extended holding pattern I was feeling queasy, but managed to "overcome" through touchdown (whenever airborne, Dad always maintained a vigil, ready to rescue me if green around the gills!). Once on the ground, I fully recovered, and we proceeded to enjoy our most memorable time.

Years earlier, before Mae's arrival, there was a trip where Dad, Bill, and I encountered an unexpected, severe thunderstorm in mid-flight. Our small plane was violently tossed about as lightening illuminated the sky. Dad proceeded to make an emergency landing in a field, with the farmer soon arriving at the scene and inviting us to his home. Accepting his accommodating offer, we stayed until it was deemed safe to resume our journey. Being quite young at the time I have limited memory of details, but vividly do remember the threatening sight of torrential rain and flashing lightning as we were buffeted through the air. Given there was zero visibility, I can only imagine the angel wings that were underneath and just outside my window. In all the years we flew, this was the only time we encountered emergency measures.

The Old Tin Goose had served us well. I was twelve years old when Dad placed it up for sale, intending to buy another, newer model later. For whatever reasons, however, he retired from piloting that day and I would miss, from then on, our adventures in the sky. With great nostalgia, I can still hear his voice: "This is N979276 requesting takeoff."

Chapter Four

EMBROIDERY HOOPS, COOKIE CUTTERS, AND PAPER DOLLS

I deeply respected my father. He was fun-loving and extremely interesting, along with being a kind and generous man. When among family and friends he was the life of the party, always having an amusing anecdote to recount and a hearty, contagious laugh to accompany it. I so enjoyed Dad's animated renditions, and he possessed an impressive repertoire. During my younger years, when without childcare at home, I spent many days with my dad at his machine shop, exploring and probably pestering my brother as he tinkered with his newest engine. Dad was happy in this environment, for he found great satisfaction in being productive. He was extremely adept in the machinery world, and I liked how he whistled while in the midst of his work. Losing my mother had been by far the most devastating event he had ever faced. It was so painful I learned at an early age not to bring up the subject. I so loved Dad and never wanted to see him sad. It took great determination to carve out a new life, but having two young children he did just that, rebuilding his world for all of us.

As I became a bit older, Mae mentioned one day that when she applied for the job, she asked my father if he drank, having left a prior position where alcohol was involved and not wanting to repeat the experience. Dad's response was, as she retold it, "I did, but put that behind, knowing I had two kids to raise." He had endured some extremely rough years, struggling to cope with the pain of his loss and striving to shelter his children from it … until finally clouds parted, allowing the storm to subside. Now aware of the decision he had made, I was deeply touched and proud of my father for his courage and commitment. On a lighter note, he would later express some final thoughts on the subject of imbibing, and in his usual, humorous way affirm, "The truth of the matter is, *the stuff's made to sell, not consume!*"

Lunchtime at the shop usually prompted a drive to the local Steak 'n Shake where we would eat, by way of curb service, in the car. While Dad affectionately referred to me as "Susie", my brother, Bill, was "Willie." Using these nicknames he cued us in turn to place our order. I never understood why Dad and the carhop were so amused when I stated my request for a hamburger with pickles and *keputch*. Dad must have enjoyed my inaccurate pronunciation as he never made known any need for correction. It wasn't until I was eight years old, and spending a week with cousins, that Uncle Kermit endearingly illustrated the correction by saying, "Patty, you run and I'll *catch-up.*" His efforts were a success and I never mispronounced the word again.

Mae joined our family as I was approaching third grade, and with her she brought a most welcome activity into my life. On weekends when Bill was with Dad at the shop, spending free time doing what he most enjoyed, I was with Mae at home, now a safe and secure haven. Of course I still had friends I played with often, but Mae introduced me to a craft that I quickly came to appreciate. Teaching me how to embroider, I spent hours working on projects and delighted in creating something beautiful. Completing pairs of pillowcases, pre-stamped with floral designs, I would send these as gifts to my Aunt Ruby and Aunt Nellie for Christmas. I was eager to learn the various techniques for producing the best results, such as keeping the material taut in the hoop and making small stitches rather than large. It was a delightful, rewarding skill which Mae and I both enjoyed.

Mae's son and family also lived in Decatur. Her two granddaughters, Pattie and Sue, respectively were one and three years my senior. They spent many Saturdays at our home and we developed a close liaison. Some of the more memorable times we shared were during the Christmas season. Mae and the three of us girls would ride the bus to town, joining the hustle and bustle of other holiday shoppers. Walking through the festively decorated streets, store to store, there would often be snow flurries in the air and a ringing of the Salvation Army bell beckoning worthy donations. After a visit to Santa in Central Park, we returned home to wrap and tag our secret treasures. On a subsequent Saturday we rallied around to make old-fashioned cut-out cookies. These became a long-standing favorite, for with Mae's recipe, nearly every year since I've made these holiday treats using our original cutters. Mae, Pattie, Sue, and I would engage in a bake-off marathon, preparing several batches of dough to place in the refrigerator. Rolling out a portion at a time, we cut our various shapes, trees, bells, stars, candy canes, and gingerbread men, and then baked and cooled. Next we prepared the homemade icing, and in adding food colorings, had a festive array of choices with which to frost and decorate our creations. Our endeavors resulted in dozens of artfully appointed cookies, as well as a flour-covered kitchen!

I would often accompany Mae as she visited friends or relatives for an afternoon. Helen was her niece but more like a cousin since they were close to the same age. I enjoyed spending time in her country home as it was elegantly decorated with Victorian furniture, including a grand dining room table with buffet and a welcoming parlor with a handsome piano. We would often sit in this room during our visits, and I found it comfortable and charming. Outside there was a pleasant garden setting, and I believed this to be Helen's childhood home. It was so historic there was a hand pump for drawing water over the kitchen sink and no indoor plumbing. Visiting the outdoor plumbing was somewhat of a rustic experience, but not my first, as several rural homes at this time were still without inside facilities.

One of my best friends from third through fifth grade was Jane, whose family moved into our neighborhood when we were both eight. Jane was especially artistic and loved to draw. I, too, had an innate propensity for art, so with her influence began to develop those talents. One of our favorite activities was drawing paper dolls and designing clothes for them. We would spend hours sketching in my basement, where during hot summer days the temperature would be a full ten degrees cooler. This had also been an early playground for me as I roller-skated endlessly to my favorite childhood records. And it was here I played school, creating a makeshift classroom and luring in my students with the promise of refreshments. During this time very few homes had air conditioning, and the summer months yielded not only intense heat but also high humidity. I was delegated the task of mowing, and with a manual reel mower, completing this mission required several glasses of Mae's lemonade.

Life had stabilized on many fronts. With Mae, I began attending Foursquare Gospel Church. Dad drove us to and from the service each Sunday, and it was a wonderful reinforcement to my childhood faith. I developed some very meaningful friendships as I attended Sunday school, church, and summer vacation Bible school. I admired Rev. and Mrs. Erickson, the senior pastors, as they were so genuinely caring and devoted to the ministry. Everyone who had the privilege of knowing the Ericksons loved and deeply respected them. I'm extremely grateful for the teachings I received at this wonderful fellowship, for it resulted in a solid spiritual base throughout my adolescent years. As destiny would have it, two decades later I and my family returned to the newly named Decatur Foursquare Church where we all became members. Over the next twenty years our children were active in youth groups, and my husband and I were honored to serve in a variety of leadership roles.

School had also been reinforced, for Mae prepared food for the annual fall festival and attended parent-teacher conferences. In addition, she came for classroom visitation, *arriving so neatly dressed and smiling, as she graciously and quietly slipped to the back of the room to be seated.*

Chapter Five

Moon Shadows

Throughout fourth and fifth grades Jane and I continued a wonderful friendship, spending the summer months drawing and playing Monopoly. When not in retreat of the basement, we were likely playing jacks on the porch, jumping rope, or riding bikes around the playground. Somewhere in this time frame the hula hoop came on the scene, making quite a splash in kids' entertainment. The fad of the day, we became quite accomplished and could keep it twirling at high speed around our neck, arms, wrists, waist, legs, and ankles. It was actually a great exercise regimen, although that was of no concern to us, for we were just having fun and honing our proficiency!

I was very inclined toward academics and the continued diversities of learning. If apprehensive about an upcoming test I earnestly prayed over the matter. After preparing to the best of my ability I then felt serene peace, placing all confidence in God's provision. By now I had a well-established prayer life and a committed relationship with Jesus. A supreme anchor, I continued to grow in His truths and love Him all the more.

Before going to sleep and as I lay in bed, the moon was a perfect nightlight glowing down through my bedroom window. I gazed at the mysterious shadows, curious as to what they were so high in the sky and far away. Moreover, I pondered heaven, wondering of its place in the midst of this universe.

I talked to God about many things, from school, to friends, to even my mother. The one and only time I inquired about her, Dad painfully told me she was ill in a hospital. Upon my request to visit, there was a gentle but negative response. Eventually, I learned she had suffered a mental breakdown and medication, often experimental and dangerous in that era, had significantly intensified the problem. As a result, she was institutionalized and it became a tragedy of the times, given the very poor status of medical and therapeutic assistance for psychological difficulties. I never knew the specifics of what my mother suffered from or through, and, as a child, only had awareness that she was ill, in a hospital, and I was unable to see her.

Because I was a baby when our mother was taken, I was not nearly so affected as Bill. Undoubtedly, my six-year-old brother felt significant trauma in so tragically losing his mother. I would not miss to that degree something I had never known. At the same time, I felt a deep love for my mom, along with sadness that she was sick and in any state of suffering. By nature I was a happy child, but when I thought of her I would become emotional and wish, somehow, I could help my mom get well again. An inborn love for one's mother is also cause for her defense. One day, the neighborhood gang was out playing and as kids will be kids, someone yelled, "Your mom's crazy!" Feeling very protective, I yelled back doubly loud, "You just shut up! She is not!" I guess that was about the best defense a seven-year-old could muster up!

By all accounts my mother was very beautiful, talented, and lovely in every way. As a child I would spend hours looking through photo albums in my father's dresser drawer. There I found and cherished pictures of my mom and dad in their early years of marriage, admiring the very handsome couple they made. Portrayed was a history of the places they lived during my father's work travels. I imagined those years to be ones of excitement and adventure as they resided in the east coast cities. My aunt Nellie and cousin Helen were just young girls when my parents returned home for visits on the farm. At the time, my grandparents lived in a three-story, red brick country home, so my dad and mom had their very own room. Years later, Nellie and Helen conveyed how my mother was so kind and gracious in allowing them to play at her dressing table, as they found it a very special treat to survey all the make-up and hair accessories.

In the dresser drawer I also found memorabilia of my mother's high school years, for she and my dad were married just after her graduation. A report card revealed she was a straight-A student and drawings depicting athletics confirmed her artistic talent. In addition, she was named on a playbill as one of the cast members in her high school theatrical production. I loved learning everything I could about her, and my dad's dresser drawer was a gateway of enlightenment. I so admired this wonderful woman I had discovered. She was my mother of whom I was proud and would forever deeply love.

In those solemn moments with the moon looking down, my prayer was God help her wherever she was. Then, picturing my mom holding me close, in a blanket of love I whispered, "good night."

Chapter Six

The Colors of Autumn

As summer months would unfold into fall and another school year was well into session, the newly arrived season created its own special memories. Along the block south of our home were older two-story houses where towering maples lined the boulevard. How gloriously they stood in their autumn attire, a vibrant array of red, yellow, and orange. With winter approaching the palate of colors would gracefully turn brown, preparing for the cold and snowy months ahead. Amidst a blanket of leaves, I kicked through the fallen and rustling mounds while walking to my friend's for an afternoon of play.

In the '50s, trick-or-treating was a highlight of the year, this being an era when parents felt secure about the safety of their children as they were enjoying an evening of fun. Groups of us traversing house to house in masquerade were cheerily greeted and invited inside, neighbors good-heartedly attempting to guess our identities. Rewarded with treats, we then progressed onward to repeat the adventure. It was a magical and enchanting event as we shuffled through leaves at night, streetlamps and glowing windows illuminating our way. We delighted in the festive décor upon each porch as scarecrows, cornstalks, pumpkins, or jack-o-lanterns were there to greet us and celebrate the season. By the end of the evening, bags filled with delights, we all returned home to survey and enjoy our acquisitions.

Safety and security helped define the times and as the decade ended, it was forever lost in a new and developing realm. Throughout my childhood we seldom locked doors when leaving the house, as crime in neighborhoods scarcely existed. Neighbors often left keys in the ignitions while cars were parked in front of their homes. At the end of the day, I had no recollection over those many years of anyone I knew being affected by theft.

One memorable autumn, Mae's sister-in-law, Amy, whom we were visiting in a neighboring small town, drove the three of us to a local orchard where we each enjoyed picking a basketful of apples. An especially serene and peaceful surrounding, it was one of those soul-touching, experiential moments. I'm fully aware it was among God's ways of speaking to my heart through the magnificence of nature. As a result of our venture, we enjoyed a variety of Mae's culinary treats: apple pies, applesauce, and apple butter.

This was also the time of year for wiener roasts, hayrides, and bobbing for apples. I fondly recall such an evening when attending a party sponsored by Awana, an outreach ministry for children. This worthy program offered fun and fellowship while incorporating a wonderful format of sharing the Bible and memorizing scripture. For nearly two years I enjoyed the weekly sessions of Awana Club at the nearby Riverside Baptist Church, and these became yet another significant addition to my spiritual growth.

Autumn held a very special place in my childhood as it provided a season filled with fun and festivities …. But it was the vision of glorious maples, leaves drifting softly to the ground, and an orchard filled with ripened apples that remained paramount. This was nature at its best, with God being the Master Artist. Each year for Arbor Day, my school gave every student a sapling to take home for planting. I was always eager and excited assisting Dad, as we gave my tiny trees a welcome new life in our yard or boulevard. Over the years I watched them grow strong and tall. Now, a half century later, I imagine their beauty in the fall, as some young child enjoys the wonder of the season and shuffles through their fallen leaves.

Chapter Seven

UNDER WESTERN SKIES I

Early in my fourth-grade year Dad designed a project wherein he and Bill would construct a family camper. In his wisdom he purposed to create some enjoyable, educational experiences as well as lasting and meaningful memories … all in the great outdoors. In their free time they worked several months toward this goal, welding, framing, sawing, and nailing, and I too spent portions of many weekends sharing in the progress. Finally brought to completion, we had a small housing unit substantially secured on an International truck bed. The interior provided beds, a sink, a small refrigerator, and room for storage. Our new rig would accommodate us with two delightful and rewarding western vacations.

With the arrival of summer, we were ready for our maiden voyage. The plan was to drive to Colorado Springs where Mae would stay and visit with family while Dad, Bill, and I continued on with a planned itinerary. Following our vacation we would then reunite and make the trip home.

It was heartwarming to see Clarence and Ruth again. With Mae at her destination, the three of us began our adventures by riding the cog rail to the Pike's Peak summit and back. From there we traveled through the beautiful and magnificent Rocky Mountain National Park as we began a northwesterly trek toward the state of Washington where Dad wanted to visit the Grand Coulee Dam. It was a time of togetherness, with Dad driving, me in the middle, and Bill on the other side. My brother was the quiet, low maintenance one while I was the more talkative question box. Intermittently we would exchange conversation, perhaps on a point of interest or the beauty of the landscape, but as Dad enjoyed a good measure of quiet time, we would often just relax and be left to our own thoughts.

Dad loved the West, a striking contrast to the large cities in which he had lived and worked during his younger years. As time passed, he much preferred wide open spaces over the more congested metropolitan areas. Not surprisingly, except for our trip to Florida with Grandpa, each of our vacations had a western destination.

The Grand Coulee Dam in its magnitude was both interesting and educational, but especially for Dad and Bill it was a source of great enjoyment as they, in detail, accessed the intricacies of its inner workings. Gravitating toward anything engine-powered, a thorough review and discussion would usually result before the subject was left behind. One might guess I would have gleaned some portion of this knowledge, given the conversations to which I was privy, but I can hardly state that to be even partially true!

As we traveled southward, I especially enjoyed an archeological museum in Utah where the skeletal structure of a dinosaur had been discovered embedded in rock. The tour was fascinating and included several other artifacts on display. This was an engaging landscape, as the mountainous red rock formations were, again, a very different portrait from that of the Midwest. It was peak vacation season and interesting to note the many other campers on the highway. Represented was everything from the homemade rig such as ours to an old converted school bus to the deluxe silver Airstream.

Driving along, Dad would sometimes interject an educational fact, affirming on one occasion, "The automobile was a marvelous invention. When pioneers crossed the West in covered wagons, they were fortunate to complete ten miles per day." This of course was an object lesson in history. In another instance regarding heat reflection, he said, "Susie, see that standing water on the road up ahead? You watch it and tell me when we get there." Consistently a disappearing act, it served as a lesson in the refraction of light.

We were getting the routine down pretty well. At times we cooked breakfast over a campfire, frying bacon and eggs in a skillet, while on other days we prepared a sandwich lunch. In between our culinary endeavors there were also the more-than-inviting cafes. Paramount to our success, the camper provided a safe haven and comfortable night's rest. Especially memorable were evening walks through the campgrounds where we were often surrounded by towering ponderosas and the scent of fresh pine. The night skies were spectacular, so huge and clear and with stars all the way to the horizon. I only remember a single negative event in this otherwise totally delightful experience. One afternoon we pulled into a campground and I proceeded to the washroom. For whatever reason, the overseer, who had registered our entry, followed me, inquiring as to the whereabouts of my mother. Still a question mark in my mind, this was an extremely sensitive topic and I felt very uncomfortable being confronted with it, especially by a stranger. Visibly shaken, I simply retreated, briskly returning to our campsite and never mentioning the incident.

Traveling the mountain highway with its panoramic views, we continued to our next destination, Nevada's Hoover Dam. A monumental structure, Dad and Bill once more were in their element, analyzing the various aspects of construction. Even I had to admit it was an impressive sight. Resuming our journey, Mae would soon be onboard as we embarked upon the final leg of our trip, heading home.

Following our return I looked forward to Vacation Bible School. I thought of Dad and how he and my mother had attended church years earlier. I learned that following her departure, Dad could not bring himself to go alone as it brought back memories too painful to bear. Yet he was ever the defender of Christianity and the moral virtues therein. Also, more than willing to provide us transportation to church, he gave it priority.

I deeply appreciated Dad and understood why he was drawn to the West. The majestic pine-covered mountains, fragrant clean air, and spacious blue skies were a wonderful feeling of tranquility.

Chapter Eight

UNDER WESTERN SKIES II

Albeit rookies, we had joined ranks with the campers of America. Last year's venture was such a success that Dad planned another to which we looked forward with great anticipation. This trip, Mae would keep the home fires burning while we, once again, wandered the western frontier. She too would be on vacation, enjoying time with friends or just relaxing.

The camper packed, we were in the cab as we waved goodbye to Mae on a sunny June morning. Dad had set a course that would take us to destinations in South Dakota, Montana, and Wyoming. Settling into the drive ahead, we were now northwestern bound.

Jane's family was moving as her father's promotion would soon relocate them to the Chicago area. We would miss each other and all the good times we shared but promised to write and send drawings too. Cindy was my oldest longtime friend and now that we were older, we especially enjoyed just being together, and riding our bicycles around the school playground. We had first met as toddlers when Aunt Icie and her mother shared neighborly chats while hanging out their wash. The Lehmans lived just around the corner, so our backyards were adjoining. Aunt Icie would pass me over the white picket fence to play in the kiddie pool with Cindy and Greg. Mrs. Lehman was so kind to me throughout my childhood and Cindy and I, almost like sisters, developed a friendship that would last a lifetime.

Mt. Rushmore was our first major attraction. Truly a wonder, I still consider it the most memorable of monuments. One cannot witness such a work of genius without having it indelibly "carved" in her mind. Our next goal was to reach Montana's grand Glacier National Park. Among Dad's favorites, Bill and I would soon learn why as we experienced its grandeur for ourselves. Enveloped by towering ponderosas and breathtaking mountains, this present setting seemed beyond compare. Once again, the western sky was compellingly blue, clear, and enormous as it too appeared especially picturesque and unparalleled. The overlooks provided a spectacular panorama, and each bend in the road brought a unique new vantage point. At one stop we were greeted by a colony of chipmunks so tame they ate from our hands. Tapping into our snacks, we enjoyed these amusing little creatures, ensuring they were all well fed before our departure. Encountering snow remaining from winter, we also enjoyed tossing a few snowballs in June. At the current altitude we were now wearing jackets to stay warm.

Camping at nightfall was an adventure in the senses. A black velvet backdrop, the sky was a masterpiece sparkling with diamonds and the pine mountain air was invigoratingly fragrant. Mindful that bears were local inhabitants, we also purposed to be ever vigilant. A spectacular sunrise would greet us each morning as we awakened and prepared for the day. Back on the highway, winding along one morning, we pulled off the road to enjoy beautiful St. Mary's Lake. There was a large rocky approach, and in running, I fell, causing a fairly deep cut on my knee. Dad, equipped with first aid, tended to the wound, and fortunately there were no complications. Only a scar remains to this day, serving as a souvenir.

I could certainly appreciate Dad's partiality, for in all the magnificence we had previously seen this had been unsurpassed. We were now on our way to Yellowstone as we traveled the final stretches of Glacier's highway. Enjoying the splendor I took snapshots in my mind, wanting to remember it forever.

When school resumed I would be in my last year at Riverside. This historic institution had been a vital part of our lives, Bill and I first attending when we were each in kindergarten. Living next door, I was privileged to have it as a convenient play area. My friends and I enjoyed several years of riding bikes and roller skating around the grounds, as well as shooting hoops and playing on the jungle gyms. With the first grade classrooms facing the side of our home, we were just a stone's throw away from the school building. By way of Mrs. Lehman, Cindy told me in latter years about my mother's last day at home. In his first-grade classroom Bill left his desk, more than once walking to the window to gaze down at the house. In each instance the teacher went to him, gently taking his hand and leading him back to his seat. As I imagine what my brother was feeling that day, my eyes still tear. Clearly, he knew his life would be drastically changing.

Bill not only inherited Dad's ingeniousness as it pertained to mechanical aptitude, but he had plenty of his own as well. Given a couple of motors when he was very young, he thoroughly examined and enjoyed them as toys. At age twelve he dismantled the car engine, then studied the various parts, and reassembled to perfection. His supreme knowledge and talents would provide him a secure and more than successful lifelong career.

Yellowstone National Park was fascinating and unique unto itself. With Old Faithful, the Morning Glory Pool, numerous bubbling mud pots, and spewing geysers, not much else could compare! We marveled as we walked the boardwalk, passing the many unusual, even bizarre geological phenomena, and we spent an extended time appreciating this one-of-a-kind landmark. Our drive through the expanse of Yellowstone was a great connection in wildlife. From the safety of our truck we had front row seats as we observed several bears at close range. A herd of buffalo was in the grassland to the right and we saw a gathering of antelope as well as a random moose. This was big game country and a marvelous grand finale.

Our second adventure at camping had proven another success, creating a storehouse of new and cherished memories. While Dad had taken numerous pictures with his camera, I had taken my own in my mind. I would later transfer one to canvas, presenting to him my rendition of Glacier National Park. The painting hung in my father's office, above his desk, until the day he retired.

Chapter Nine

FAREWELL RIVERSIDE

Mr. Stricklin, stocky and well-rounded, had a most pleasant demeanor and was my only male teacher throughout attendance at Riverside. Upon entering sixth grade, our class was now at the top of the totem pole. This year I had been awarded the honor and title of "Flag Girl." Each morning before school I raised the American flag to the top of the pole in the northeast corner of the playground. Likewise, after school was dismissed I lowered it, and with an assistant, neatly tri-folded and stored so the procedure could be repeated.

Riverside, constructed in the late 1890s, was a classic and historic three-story, red brick schoolhouse. A stately structure, it featured four chimneys projecting from the roofline, tall windows positioned in rows around the entire perimeter, and a grand front entrance, as well as entry from the back. The interior boasted of creaking hardwood floors and two commanding staircases.

In the basement was the PTA room where special meetings and conferences were held. There was a movie projector at the back facing a standing white screen at the front. Folding chairs were placed in rows with a middle aisle down the length of the room. Each year at the beginning of the holiday season, Mr. Keys, our principal, would instruct one or two classes per session to file downstairs for an annual viewing of *The Night Before Christmas*. There was always excitement in the air as the lights switched off and the reel began turning, its rhythmic hum accompanying the animated classic.

On the first floor, with a large open space in the middle, classrooms were located in the outer circumference, one in each corner. There was a kindergarten room, two first grades, and one sixth grade, with the school office next to it, and at the top of the stairs near the main entrance. Located on the second story, with the same basic floor plan, were the second, third, fourth, and fifth grade classrooms. During my years at Riverside the third level was inaccessible to students, most likely being used as storage. Perhaps in prior years the school had served an expanded number of grades.

One of the unique features of these vintage schoolhouses was the cloak room, a narrow hallway parallel to each class. Here, during the winter season, students would hang their coats, hats, scarves, and leggings on the rows of hooks provided. Boots would also be removed and lined along the wall. As it had its own doorway from the large open room, students would enter from there, removing outer clothing and continuing through an archway to their class on the opposite side.

Every classroom contained some consistent elements. With very high ceilings, several lights, each with the classic schoolhouse globe, hung from long extensions and were evenly spaced throughout. A large blackboard spanned the front of the room, and above its length was a border displaying the small and upper case alphabet. Strikingly, two large portraits, one each of George Washington and Abraham Lincoln, were displayed on adjacent walls. The American flag held its own place of honor. Beginning each day, right hands over our hearts, we stood to face it, reciting together "The Pledge of Allegiance."

Riverside Grade School provided a warm and wonderful familiarity, as it became a very special and endearing part of our lives. I had segued from kindergarten to sixth grade, now progressing through my final year at this beloved institution, one which would serve the generations over a span of eighty years. Then, one ill-fated day it met with the wrecking ball, when by the dictate of "progress" a new housing development was to occupy the property. As I was no longer living next door or even in the area, Cindy so thoughtfully recovered two bricks, one for each of us, from the wreckage. It was a worthy and treasured keepsake by which to remember our alma mater.

Countless days Cindy and I rode bikes around the playground of Riverside. As we were now getting older, she soon to be in eighth grade and I in seventh, my first year of junior high, we enjoyed the opportunity of just being together to talk. Amidst a wide range of topics, we agreed on how dreamy was Adam of *Bonanza*! Embracing ten years of friendship, Cindy and I had passed the test of time. We had enjoyed walks, making hollyhock dolls from flowers along the alley, and gathering mulberries from the tree next to my garage. When even younger, we gathered buckeyes from a rare tree in our neighborhood. We were intrigued with the unusual fruit and gathered it from the ground as if a precious treasure. Over the years Cindy and I developed an ongoing history, always reconnecting even when lapses of time occurred. One day, when we were adults, she said, "Patty, I never knew anyone so resilient as you." I had never thought of it that way, but with God in my life, I realized there had been a supernatural resiliency.

My father and mother's 1934 wedding portrait

My brother, Bill, and me in 1950

… And with my mother

The Old Tin Goose in 1951, ready for a flight to Indiana

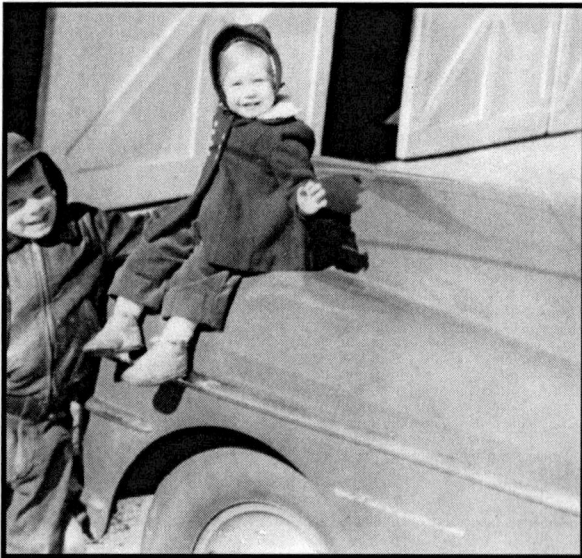

Bill and me before departure

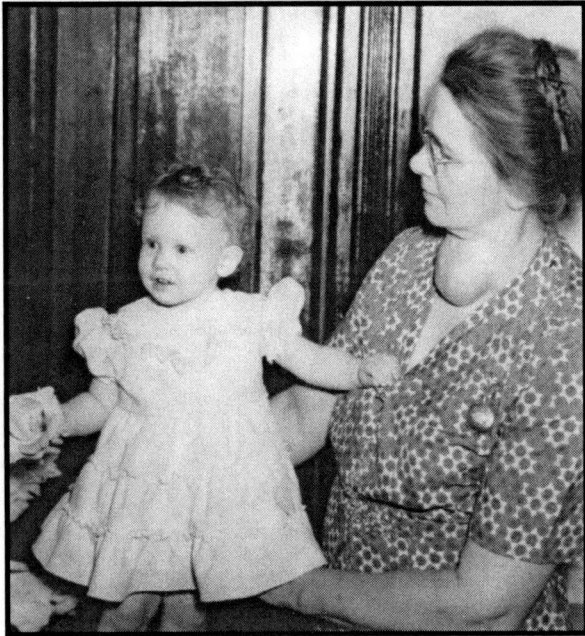

With Aunt Icie after arriving at my grandparents'

Grandpa and Grandma Christian

Bill and me at the shop,
inspecting his Maytag motor in 1953

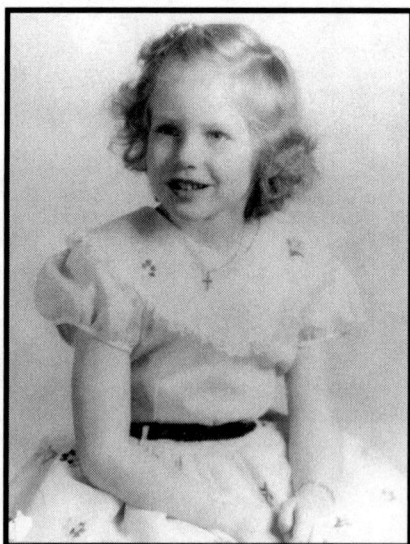

1954 studio portrait arranged by Mildred

All the gang for Giggy's birthday in 1956. Greg in front,
l-r Cindy, David, Bill, me, Linda, and Cheryl

First grade class with Mrs. Brown. Greg in back, standing
2nd from right, and I'm 3rd from left in middle row

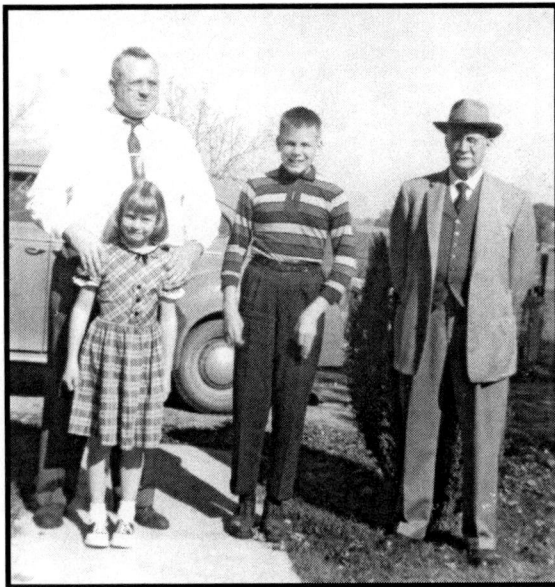

Dad, me, Bill, and Grandpa
Indiana circa 1957

Mae in the back yard
next to some of her beautiful flowers
circa 1959

Prior to departing an Indiana reunion in 1959. Mae, Aunt Nellie, and Aunt Ruby with a few of us cousins, Mike, me, Susie, and Sherry

Fourth grade class with Mrs. Fielder. Jane and
I on chairs 4th and 5th from left

Riverside Grade School in 1960. The back side facing our home

Chapter Ten

Expanding Horizons

My Indiana relatives, with the love and wonderful memories they provided, added a vital and secure element to my childhood. This was my dad's side of the family. Grandpa and Grandma Christian had four children: two sons and two daughters. Dad's siblings included Uncle Chet, Aunt Ruby, and Aunt Nellie and, later, correlating spouses were Aunt Etta, Uncle Floyd, and Uncle Kermit. From there, several cousins completed the family tree. Since my Aunt Icie was a great-aunt, being Grandma's brother's wife, I saw her more infrequently, treasuring the opportunity when it did arise. At the age of six, when saying goodbye at one of our reunions, Aunt Ruby lovingly suggested that I write to her and that she would write back. Always taking seriously any promise or proposal, I wrote her a letter soon after and she indeed reciprocated. As with others in the family, Aunt Ruby and I began a close correspondence, one that would continue over the next forty years.

My mother was an only child and my maternal grandmother passed away before I knew her. Grandpa Shewman was remarried, so I had a step-grandmother. They were the only relatives on my mother's side of the family, or at least that I ever met, and I only recall visiting them on one occasion. When I was seven Dad flew me to their home in Michigan where I stayed for a week. During my visit it seemed there was very little relational interaction, and in fact I remember being lonely. I was so happy when Dad returned, feeling wonderfully safe and warm as I sat next to him on the plane trip home. Additionally, Dad had a surprise. As he led me to the garage and lifted the overhead door, there was my first, brand new bicycle! It was a beautiful aqua blue with a second seat on the back and streamers extending from the handle grips. I loved my bike and would ride it a gazillion times around the playground of Riverside Grade School.

Now, having recently celebrated my twelfth birthday, I would soon be in the seventh grade and attending a new school, Johns Hill Junior High. It was located a few blocks away and on a steep incline within Johns Hill Park. I needed to allow time for the walk, since it would be quite different from crossing an alley to Riverside. This would be an exciting venture and an opportunity to make friends from other schools, as we all merged into a new milestone.

I quickly adjusted to the concept of lockers, changing classrooms, having several teachers, and eating lunch at school. In fact, the pace was so much faster-moving, the day seemed to fly by quickly. Probably due in part to my unconventional childhood, I was now a bit on the bashful side and somewhat lacking in confidence. Focused on academics, I would shy away from clubs and extracurricular activities. I was tenacious, however, with a strong desire to learn and succeed. Rewardingly, my efforts kept me at honor roll status throughout both years of junior high.

It was here in seventh grade that I first met Adele, as she had previously attended Southeast. We soon became very close friends and would remain so throughout high school. Adele was the one to initiate our friendship, which was quite an honor as she was relatively popular and outgoing. Her parents both worked in major department stores, so she was always stylishly dressed, possessing an impressive wardrobe. She invited me for occasional sleepovers and I admired her more-than-comfortable, well-appointed home, as well as the fact that she had her very own room. Mae and I shared a bedroom, so to have this much personal space and privacy seemed quite a luxury. Adele and I spent portions of many weekends together, enjoying girl-talk, baking cookies, or looking at fashion magazines. She and I developed a wonderful friendship, and I was honored with the respect and loyalty I felt from her, as did she from me. Her mother, on occasion, would bring us carryout pizza, my first introduction to this trendy new treat. The two of us shared several classes, so we studied together, talked about boys, the latest clothes fashions and, overall, confided in one another about most everything. Life had taken a quantum leap forward, and the teenage years were rapidly approaching. At this juncture, a good and fiercely loyal friend was a major blessing.

I enjoyed each of my seventh-grade classes which included science, math, English, history, home economics, and physical education. Regarding the latter, I wasn't overly athletic but could hold my own. Mr. Fritz, my science teacher, was exceptional in his knowledge of the subject matter as well as in presentation and interpersonal skills. Interesting and comprehensive, he was also very kind, soon making him my favorite teacher and science my favorite subject of the year.

He arranged two special events for our class which became especially memorable. Early one Saturday morning we departed for a fieldtrip to Chicago, touring the Natural History Museum and the Museum of Science and Industry. The fascination and magnitude of both would stay with me for months to come. Secondly, we were required to prepare a special project for exhibit at the annual science fair. Mr. Fritz suggested I demonstrate the subject of "plant propagation." In garnering my teacher's advice and reviewing the relevant material, I designed a tri-fold backboard with documented script as well as graphics to illustrate the various points. In addition, I had several plants growing in painted green cans of various shapes and sizes, these being the propagating systems described. Unforgettable was the morning we departed, as I boarded the bus juggling several canned plants, a large backboard, a sack lunch, and my purse. I finally made it to my seat, everything in tow, as did all the other students with their creative efforts. Reaching our destination, we set up our displays in the designated area and waited for judging. At the conclusion, we were each rewarded with a worthy recognition. In his career field Mr. Fritz was stellar, bringing not only education to the classroom, but also curiosity, inspiration, and achievement.

Eighth grade followed suit as I thrived on learning and rising to the various challenges. I welcomed the independence and responsibilities of time management. Even lunch was an event, friends gathering to purchase menu selections and then chatting together while sitting on the gym bleachers to eat. I enjoyed my ever-growing peer group and was gaining a sense of comfort and confidence in this graduated environment. My life had substantially expanded since days at Riverside, which now seemed a long time ago.

We all remember where we were when we first heard the news of John F. Kennedy's assassination. On that November day in 1963, I was in my eighth-grade, seventh-hour study hall when the principal's voice came over the intercom announcing our president's death. It was a tragedy that impacted us each, as students were home, dismissed from school and watching the unfolding televised events. At the capitol rotunda, and in the forefront, were First Lady Jacqueline Kennedy and her two young children, Caroline and John Junior. As the horse-drawn casket was transported to Arlington National Cemetery, we were affixed to the somber procession. A grievous day in history, the gravity and depth of it were felt by even the youngest of us.

On the upbeat side, a few months later The Beatles landed on American soil, deplaning in February of '64 for their grand debut on the Ed Sullivan show. Once again we were glued to the television, but this time in anticipation of a well-promoted performance. Every girl, including me, had her favorite Beatle, and mine, along with that of ten million others, was Paul. The four mop tops successfully launched a singing sensation that night, as they belted out their first immortalized hit, "I Want to Hold Your Hand." This was the beginning of Beatlemania and I was smack in the middle!

In junior high I began attending the Foursquare church alone. Unaware of details, I only knew there was some kind of "tiff" between Dad and Mae regarding transportation, resulting in her decision to remain at home. Dad would drive me to church, and following the service I walked the few blocks to his shop. Sometime thereafter, we then returned home where Mae would have Sunday dinner. My faith had been a foundation and it was certain throughout my childhood that God had always been with me protecting and guiding my life. Expanded into new and contrasting elements, how much more would I now need His guidance and grace?

- Chapter Eleven -

E_{HS}

By the fall of 1964 teenagers everywhere were singing along with The Beatles, Herman's Hermits, the Supremes, and more by way of their transistor radios. This, of course, was during free time when not in school or studying.

I was now a freshman at EHS, home of the Eisenhower Panthers. Eisenhower was a relatively new building, modernly designed and on one level ... quite a contrast to my previous schools. I would walk several blocks before arriving to homeroom, my first connection of the day and where attendance was taken. Here in G-100, Coach Alexander was our homeroom teacher all four years. Being our celebrated football coach, we enjoyed the unique and upbeat atmosphere he brought to the classroom. Routine matters were approached much the same as those on the field. Coach would call on us by our last name only and in a coach tone of voice, but with an energy that always made us smile. He presented a no-nonsense kind of demeanor, which was accompanied by an unsurpassed wit and twinkle in his eye. As the years unfolded, I also had Coach for senior English where his signature animations brought delight to all of us throughout a year of Shakespeare. In the midst of a lecture he characteristically paced the floor, occasionally hopping onto his desk and into a squatting position as he brought emphasis to a particular point—all while intermittently chewing his gum with great deliberation. Most likely, this was the mode of operation when briefing the team before a game! We loved Coach Alexander and learned a great deal from him that year in senior English. Freshman homeroom, however, was our first introduction to this creative style of teaching, and we thought it very cool that not only he chewed gum, but allowed us to do so as well. This was quite a privilege, for in any other class it was considered a serious offense, right along with throwing paper wads!

My schedule included the standard freshman courses, and I soon developed a comfortable routine as apprehension gave way to familiarity and confidence in my new surroundings. Locker stops were strategically planned so I would arrive to my destinations on time and, for the most part, I thoroughly enjoyed each of my classes. There were those occasional challenges, such as dissecting the frog in biology, but, together, my lab partner and I successfully rose to the occasion!

While school had always been a good place in my life, I was reminded of Dad and some of the tales he would tell of school days in his youth. It seemed that he and his brother were quite the pranksters, as such endeavors were more to their liking than those of a confined classroom and studious nature. Their ill-fated destiny was not only due to the mischief itself and getting caught, but also to the fact that my grandpa, *their father,* was the school principal! There were three strikes against them as they faced the teacher, the principal, and then Grandpa again when they returned home. Maybe Dad's scholarly experience just got off to a bad start, as when he was younger there was an older girl in this country schoolhouse who mercilessly taunted him. Finally deciding to take matters into his own hands, he gave her a good kick, but regardless of the circumstance, this, of course, was deemed unacceptable. As he told the story years later in his amusing, gregarious way, he still believed the girl needed kicking and he had done the right thing! Grandpa was on the stern side, probably a necessity given his disciplinary duties both at home and school, while Grandma was the kindest, gentlest, most hardworking soul one could ever meet. I learned from my cousin Helen that Grandma prepared a large meal every Sunday after church, when her five brothers and their families joined her and Grandpa for dinner. From their poultry on the farm, she served platters of fried chicken, accompanied by several side dishes and fresh-baked pies. On another occasion, my cousin Doris endearingly stated that Grandma Christian was the sweetest, most perfect person she had ever known.

The summer following my freshman year I began working in my father's office, addressing and stuffing envelopes as I prepared them for mailing. These contained promotional materials featuring a product he had patented. His "Deco Anchor" was a device for anchoring large machinery, and its innovative design significantly made the efforts of the installer easier. I had a large reference book of nationwide industry listings, including engineers to whom I directed the material. As Dad had wisely suggested, I enrolled in a typing course the previous summer. This proved a most worthy endeavor, not only for work, but also for school as teachers preferred typewritten over handwritten reports. We weren't scheduled for typing until later in the curriculum, so having this skill my freshman year proved to be a real advantage.

An eventful sophomore year included the removal of dental braces (which had been acquired two years prior), my first pair of contact lenses and, later, a driver's permit following student training. Also in this rite of passage was my induction into a high school sorority. I and others had been submitted as candidates for Mu Delta Tau, and we soon embarked upon the humbling, but mostly fun and good natured, experience of initiation. We had weekly meetings, progressing through the pledging phase and showing proper respect to our "superiors." The final week we were paraded through town dressed like babies, and the final evening given a one-on-one specific command, mine being "Fry like bacon." Following this, and for the grand finale, an unsavory concoction was dispensed over our heads. We each "graduated" that night and were officially inducted into membership with a gala slumber party to follow. Being a member involved weekly meetings, occasional parties, and an embracing of our sisterhood. Pattie, who had submitted my candidacy and been my "big sister," was already driving and would pick me up, announcing her arrival with the sorority honk. Several friendships, including those from other schools, were made through Mu Delta Tau, and I remained a member for two years.

One sad note during my sophomore year was the passing of Grandpa. He had been ill for a while but lived to be eighty-eight. Residing with my aunt and uncle, he was finally moved to a nursing home in order to receive the needed care. I remember our last visit. After spending a period of time together, Dad gave him a firm handshake and said in a slightly trembling voice, "You take care." Trying to remain composed, his face red, I saw the same pain as when I had asked about my mother all those years ago. Not long after, we returned to Indiana for the funeral and together, as a family, paid tribute to our beloved father and grandfather.

My driver's license opened up a wonderful new element of freedom and opportunity. Adele or I would pick the other up on given evenings, often visiting Carnegie Library to gather needed reference materials for school. This was another historic and grand old institution, spacious, artfully designed, and with a unique, inviting upper level. Once our assignments were complete, we engaged in what teenagers enjoyed doing, cruising on Eldorado and through the Steak 'n Shake. Waving to friends, listening to songs on the radio, and just being light and carefree were a signature part of our youth.

Although during my high school years I failed to attend church regularly, I remained in my faith and love for God. This was a priceless and powerful element during a time when multiple distractions were present, all vying for a young person's mind. I am fully aware that my spiritual grounding kept and protected me throughout these somewhat tumultuous years.

There were also some problems at home. Seemingly, Mae was struggling with the fact that I was no longer a child, and possibly even felt intimidated now that two women were living in the same house. I loved her dearly, but without the skills to deal with issues constructively, things were just not pleasant at times. Nevertheless, given her difficult life, she had done well. Moreover, she had brought us a host of positive changes while providing for our basic needs and loving us the best she could. For this I would be forever grateful and, in fact, we remained close throughout the years to come, even as I had children of my own and until, in her eldest years, she moved away to live near her granddaughters.

Compassionately, Dad gave me a gasoline credit card along with the privilege of driving his Newport, while he and Bill drove the company truck. With understanding Dad had affirmed my situation, and in his warmhearted way he always made known how welcome I was at the shop.

As a junior and in my second year of Spanish, I especially enjoyed foreign language and being a member of Spanish Club. I also became an assistant to our school nurse, Miss Matthews. This entitled me to trade out a study hall in order to fulfill my duties. I was responsible for keeping a registry of attending patients, which most often meant allowing a student with a headache or other minor illness to retire in one of the rooms, each with a cot. I enjoyed serving in this capacity while also completing a reasonable amount of homework. Especially memorable, too, was Mr. Geer, my assigned guidance counselor. Kind and caring, he readily offered assistance if help was ever needed. Throughout our high school meetings, I enjoyed our positive chats and well remember at their close his consistent and genuine good wishes for having a wonderful day. His sincerity and encouraging nature always put an extra bounce in my step.

Another school year of continued good memories and ongoing friendships was nearing an end. Since junior high I had come into my own sense of style. Linda, whom I had first met there and now sat behind in homeroom, made the comment, as school was ending for summer, that she couldn't believe my transformation ... The awkward duckling had surely blossomed! Cindy and I still found time to connect, but with all the extracurricular events we were often both occupied within our own grades. The last three years seemed to pass in a flash and I could barely believe that we, in G-100, would soon be entering our senior year.

- Chapter Twelve -

THE GOLDEN THREAD

It was the summer of '67 and I was driving the Newport while listening to WLS on the radio. Working at Dad's, going shopping, or just out for a coke, it was great having the car keys. Occasionally Pattie stopped by inviting me to join her in an errand, and other times Cindy and I ran next door or talked on the phone. There were also weekend dates, friends getting together, and cruising with Adele.

As vacation was nearing an end, I looked forward to my senior year and "Diversified Occupations." Participating in this program, I would attend regular classes in the morning, then report to work in the afternoon. As requested, I was assigned to a dental office, having interviewed in advance with Dr. L. B. Ritter.

Back in homeroom it was good to see friends as we traded stories and returned to academics. My routine was attending school in the morning, then driving home for lunch and changing into uniform before proceeding to my workplace for the afternoon. Dr. Ritter, who was middle-aged and congenial, trained me in the various aspects of assisting, and we soon developed a wonderful working relationship. The dental facility was modern and well-arranged, including a waiting room, office, two patient rooms, an x-ray developing center, and a utility area for instrument sterilization and supply storage. There was only one "little" glitch. Irene, a well-groomed, older woman, had been the sole employee for a number of years and she clearly was not accepting this new program, much less my being a part of it. Detecting some serious territorial issues, I was determined to persevere and earn her friendship. She was also very stringent in her methods and insistent that I perform accordingly, so, in detail, I made every effort to comply. Overall, I very much enjoyed my duties and the wide spectrum they covered. Following the initial learning curve was confidence in instrument identification, x-ray development, and patient care. When present, I was chair-side assisting and attending to details in that end of the complex. Irene, essentially, was then retired to the office. Working with Dr. Ritter developed into an ongoing educational experience wherein we also enjoyed casual conversation as time allowed. Irene, on the other hand, remained a tough nut to crack as I, with intention, continued to function cheerfully around an impending cloud. Very troubling at times, I prayed that God would give me wisdom and bring resolve to the situation. As a result, I believed my responsibility was to maintain unconditional kindness.

On the school front, academics were progressing smoothly and several of us would soon be inducted into National Honor Society. An official ceremony and awards presentation was held with parents invited and Dad attended. I recognized the pride on his face and it warmed my heart. I also started dating "Mark" as we had met at a dance, he attending another school. Our relationship developed into a steady one and we began spending most of our free time together. Adele and some of my other close friends now had steadies as well, so girlfriend time had taken a back seat to this evolving, natural sequence. With a more than productive schedule and several new positive relationships, my senior year had hit a progressively comfortable stride ... until one April Friday evening.

During these years the downtown area of our city was thriving and the prime destination for retail shoppers. On Fridays the stores remained open until late in the evening, so in an ongoing pursuit of fashion, I planned to go shopping, most every girl's favorite pastime. I parked in the city garage, a few blocks from the center of town, and proceeded on my mission. After closing down the shops, parcels in hand, I was returning down the sidewalk leading to my car. A couple of blocks en route, I heard footsteps rapidly approaching from behind. The next thing I knew, there was an arm around me with a voice dictating I walk straight ahead and not make a sound as, otherwise, he had a gun and would shoot. In disbelief, I glanced back to my left in order to view the intruder. Immediately, he told me to turn back around and keep walking. I only recognized that he had on a light-colored trench coat, was fairly tall, and light in complexion. I could feel the gun pressing on my lower back, but with his left hand around my arm and walking just slightly behind, it would appear that we were together, his right hand with the gun concealed. It was one of those surreal moments where everything seemed to disconnect and begin unfolding in slow motion.

By now, the parking garage was about one quarter block away, and a strong sense came over me that I needed to break free immediately and run to my left into the street. This was a three-lane, one-way artery exiting downtown, so there were several vehicles driving in my direction. I made the break and ran, faintly aware of his command to return, and the swirl of cars around me as I made my way across a clear path to the walk on the other side. A woman and her daughter were there and I approached them, trembling and seeking help in the trauma of what had happened only moments ago. The mother, with compassion, said she had seen us but thought we were a couple together. She then feared a car would strike me as I ran into the street. Offering to walk me to safety, I gratefully accepted, thanking her several times. As we continued to the intersection, crossing back over, there was no sign of the stalker, and I was deeply grateful for the timely presence of this woman and her daughter. Safely inside my car and thanking them again, I drove to Dad's, his shop being only another two blocks away. He was in his office when I entered, still in disbelief. After relaying the incident, I believe he first called the police, but I specifically remember his decision to scour the area in an effort to locate the offender. Together, we drove along every street, looping around several times but to no avail. The guilty party was fortunate, indeed, to have eluded my father, for had he been apprehended, I suspect he would never have worried over the fate of facing a judge!

In the days following, I left school for two appointments at the police department. An artist was assigned to draw a sketch of the man according to my description. As it had been dark and I was able to glance only briefly, the information I could provide was very little. Also at the request of the authorities, I reviewed mug shots and attended a lineup but again was unable to make any positive identification.

After this incident and my quick rebound, I later wondered how I moved forward with so little residual fear. I truly believe my emotional recovery and feeling of security was rooted in God, a relationship which began with my strong commitment as a child. Although at the present time I was not as actively pursuing my spiritual walk, I was, nonetheless, eternally grateful for God's manifest love in my life and deeply cherished His presence.

Life resumed as normal, and Mark and I would soon be attending my high school prom. After I purchased the perfect gown and Mark rented a dashing tux, we enjoyed a beautiful formal evening, including dinner, Prom, and post-Prom. We had dated steadily my entire senior year, but as the summer months approached, it seemed our lives were taking different directions and we eventually drifted apart.

Now, as graduation was nearing there was a new development at work. Irene was admitted to the hospital due to an emotional breakdown. Dr. Ritter, affirming the environment had been intense, stated that she, herself, had submitted her resignation. He then inquired if I would be his fulltime assistant and office manager following graduation. I accepted his offer and then thought of Irene, feeling compassion for her at this obviously difficult time. I secured a gift and paid her a visit the following day. Expressing my sincere empathy over her situation, tears came to her eyes and she told me how sorry she was for treating me unkindly. I assured her all was forgiven, then extended a long, warm hug. Later, after returning home, she invited me to her apartment for a visit. I had finally earned her friendship and God had answered my prayer.

High school graduation was the grand finale of four years at EHS. "Pomp and Circumstance" ushered in our student procession while proud family and friends viewed from the bleachers. Commencement is always bittersweet given the joy of such a major achievement, but the end of a volume of memories. We were kids who grew up together, but would now be going our separate ways. After an inspiring ceremony, we enjoyed a celebration at home, where Mae had an array of food and several relatives were with us to enjoy it. As when Bill was the graduate, our Indiana family came to show their pride and support, and Dad, with his Polaroid camera, captured the moments for a lifetime.

It was divine appointment as I pondered Jesus and experienced a very real sense of His presence. During this window, hearts connected, God showed me the reality of His mercy and grace, a deep and abiding love that had been with and upon me all the days of my life. How was it, given the misfortunes surrounding my childhood, I managed to escape so relatively unscathed? The answer seemed crystal clear, for along with God's unfailing love there had been another key and vital element. With a child's simple faith and pure daily trust I never doubted God's love and protection. This, and my gratitude for Him, had triumphed over any earthly circumstance. With spiritual eyes I saw things in a deeper way, things I had previously taken for granted. My life, like a tapestry, was uniquely woven, and the golden thread of God's light and love had remained intact throughout.

Chapter Thirteen

DIVINE DESTINY

My job description had substantially broadened now that I was office manager as well as chair-side assistant. Nevertheless, I soon developed an organized routine and found it rewarding to maintain the necessary administrative tasks. By now, Dr. Ritter and I had a streamlined working relationship, and I was able to anticipate his needs in most any given treatment. Not only was it a pleasure working together, but also in serving our well-established clientele.

Occasionally we experienced some particularly unique situations, such as the time a patient's jaw locked following a root canal procedure. Dr. Ritter made every effort to implement the needed adjustment, but to no avail. We felt extreme empathy for the woman, knowing of her discomfort and anxiety, for she could not close her mouth from a wide-open position. As a last resort, Dr. Ritter phoned a colleague, one who was more experienced in this aspect. With his arrival and intervention, the woman was finally rescued. There was also the day we were finishing with a patient and a much-unexpected occurrence took place. As Dr. Ritter completed his work and I was standing alongside, the suspended dental equipment was suddenly set into motion and the walls and floor began moving. We all looked at one another in disbelief of what we had just seen and felt, a phenomenon that lasted about thirty seconds. After subsiding, all remained intact and we soon learned there had been a minor earthquake, the epicenter being near St. Louis, about one hundred and fifty miles south. For weeks, people were comparing notes on where they were and what they had experienced during the tremor.

By summer's end of '68, after working as a solo employee the three months prior, we acquired an additional assistant. Dr. Ritter, again, partnered with Diversified Occupations and Diane, a senior from MacArthur, came onboard while I proceeded to train her. Arriving in the afternoons she then attended to assisting, allowing me the needed time for maintaining administrative duties. Diane and I became very good friends, even getting together on days away from work. The three of us, in fact, developed a great friendship and truly enjoyed our camaraderie. One afternoon when the office was closed, DR, as we referred to him in a casual setting, treated us to a tour of the airport control tower and then a ride in his Piper Cub. Although I had flown commercially, it was nostalgic to be in a small craft again, reminding me of the days with Dad's Stinson.

During the fall I considered renting an apartment as things were still intense regarding my relationship with Mae. When I approached Dad with the idea, he was prepared to "fix" the situation, but in any case I felt this step of independence would be a good experience. In his continued wisdom he acknowledged that I wanted to "try my wings." I began exploring the possibilities, focusing on apartments near my work place, given Dad's car wasn't part of the new package! I found a promising three-room unit which was part of a large older home divided into rentals. It was unfurnished, but I saw the potential and a creative opportunity. Tapping into savings, the new furnishings and appointments brought a remarkable transformation, and there was now a warm and charming environment. I not only walked to and from work, but also the distance for shopping. Granted, this new lifestyle had a downside, including the absence of car keys, but I adjusted and dealt fairly well with the issue of inconvenience. After a few months, however, I became discouraged and a bit disillusioned for different reasons. In my naivety I had given little consideration to any negative possibilities. To my surprise, there were those who envisioned this as an ideal place to party. Never had I been involved in the alcohol or drug culture, but sadly I came to realize there were some among my peers who were. I began feeling like a prisoner, reluctant to answer the door or even the phone. Dad and I established our own calling signal, so I would know it was him and then call back. Early in the coming year I invited Dad to dinner, expressing my desire to return home. The unexpected challenges were far removed from what I had anticipated, and certainly from the reasons for which I had wanted an apartment. Apparently Dad was unsettled too, for Mae later revealed how reserved he had been during the time I was away. When I expressed concern over all the furnishings and any related complications, in an ever-ready stance of moral support, he dismissed them as only material things and nothing of actual consequence. Dad was an ongoing pillar of strength, and throughout my life I would carry his wisdom with me. The following weekend he and Bill loaded the truck, transferring the contents of my apartment to the upper level of the shop. Here they remained stored until I later sold everything, recouping what I had originally invested. It was good to be home, and I had gained worthy insight from the entire experience.

Only a few days after my return Mae came to me, expressing what she sincerely felt to be true, as if, finally, there had been some kind of inner reconciliation. Now that I was an adult, she said I should be the woman of the house and was more than capable of caring for Dad and Bill. Therefore she would be taking another position and soon begin housekeeping for an older gentleman. In those moments I tearfully hugged her a long time, and any pain and conflict there had been melted away. I did not want her to leave, but knew we would always stay closely connected. Something had given way to a returned sense of peace, and knowingness all was well once again.

Throughout the spring and summer I continued working for Dr. Ritter, and was now taking care of the household as well. This included grocery shopping and preparing dinners for my dad and brother. Unfortunate for them, they were the recipients of my early attempts at cooking! While eating our meal, Dad would inquire about my day at "the molar maulers." This was his upbeat way of showing interest in my work and encouraging conversation. During my school years the question was posed as to what I had learned at "the brain factory." Dad consistently had a good sense of humor as well as a positive attitude.

Several friends, back for the season break, had begun college while I had remained on the home front working at Dr. Ritter's. Given my high school achievements, Mr. Geer had strongly encouraged me to continue into higher education, but Dad had some opposing feelings. This was a time when many campuses were in a state of unrest, the anti-establishment, drug, and hippie movement at a pinnacle. Dad's deep concerns over these issues and his desire to protect me, naturally, became very influential. Reuniting with friends that summer of '69 was heartwarming, and among other special memories was my invitation for Dad to accompany me to *The Sound of Music.* Part of his Father's Day gift, it was a cherished time together as we enjoyed this delightful all-time favorite classic.

The following month history was made with the astronaut lunar landing and man's first steps on the moon. Televised by satellite, I paused from preparing for a date to watch this monumental event being viewed worldwide. Neil Armstrong's immortalized quote, "That's one small step for man; one giant leap for mankind," would ring throughout history. On the downbeat side the political climate was largely defined by the Vietnam War, which generated a great deal of controversy. Due to the ravages of this conflict, the toll on many of our soldiers was disheartening. Subculture protestors were ever increasing, as was a swirl of negative activity and anti-American rhetoric. Moreover, the assassination of Rev. Martin Luther King Jr. had occurred the previous year. A peaceful, heroic advocate for equal rights, it was a tragic loss during a turbulent time in our country. Politics aside, our military deserved the utmost respect and gratitude for their bravery and fight for freedom. America was the greatest nation on earth, blessed in abundance with liberty and opportunity. Not to be taken for granted, I was deeply thankful for the Christian principles upon which we had been founded and for an overall unshakable patriotism. In late summer I submitted my application to a few of the major airlines, requesting acceptance into their stewardess (later termed "flight attendant") training … a natural step given my background and love for flying. I was excited about the prospect and prayed for guidance throughout.

Then, there was that moment when I met someone who would bring clarity to my aspirations and become the significant other in our mutual destiny. By way of a friend in common, my first date with Dennis Punches was in September of 1969. Thereafter, we spent as much time together as possible. I admired how natural and genuine he was and how easily and honestly we could talk. On our first date we went jogging, both being exercise enthusiasts. I introduced him to the Eisenhower track and he introduced me to Weldon Springs where we also enjoyed boating and hiking. We shared our dreams and goals, soon realizing how much we had in common. Dennis was a Vietnam veteran whose term of duty had been completed eighteen months earlier. He had returned home safely, for which I would become increasingly and eternally grateful. After a short engagement but confident in our relationship, we were married on January 24, 1970. We had fallen in love and found our soul mate in each other. We opted to marry unconventionally, but one step short of eloping as our parents were fully aware of our intentions and timing. In large part, we felt a private ceremony, foregoing the traditional ado, would be much easier for Dad, given the absence of my mother and any related complexities. Armed with his Polaroid, Dad snapped our photo before leaving the house that day, and we then proceeded to the church where the minister had two witnesses waiting. Low-keyed and simple, it had been the right choice, and Dad's monetary gift provided a wonderful honeymoon to follow. Indeed, saying goodbye to my father was difficult and emotional, but I knew he was happy and pleased, realizing the outstanding son-in-law he was about to inherit.

In response to my application, I had since been accepted by one of the airlines, but that now paled, for I had found the love of my life and a very special part of the divine destiny for it. Little could we know when we said our vows of the plans and purposes God had, for as we would help others, *He* would help us all ... to learn, to grow, to heal ... together on this remarkable journey called *life*.

A rare photo of Adele

With my fellow nurses helpers junior year. Standing, 2nd from right

Induction into National Honor Society (1967). 2nd row, 1st on left

Diversified Occupations Club (1967-68). 1st row, far right

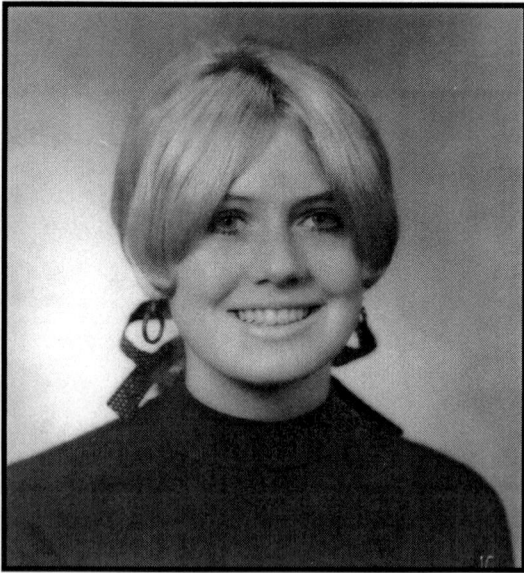

Senior picture

With Dad, prior to attending Diversified Occupations Banquet

Bill and me before graduation (May 1968)

Working with Dr Ritter (1969)

First date with Dennis, my future husband (September 1969)

Engagement portrait

Our wedding day
January 24, 1970

- Epilogue -

After we married, Dennis completed his degree and began a successful and rewarding engineering career. Following his graduation in early 1972, my mother passed away that May. During a closed-casket service our family gathered in her honor, Dad having arranged a poignant memorial. Unanswered questions remained in my mind, and there were things I would never understand this side of heaven … like why such a beautiful life had been so tragically interrupted. Paramount, however, and because of my confidence in God's promises, was the assurance that my mother was now in a realm more magnificent than I could even imagine, and once again she was happy, healthy, and vibrant. Moreover, I would finally meet her one glorious day and we would begin an eternity of love in our long-awaited union as mother and daughter. Never again to experience any pain, separation or suffering, Jesus would return, for every tear that had fallen, unspeakable joy.

Within six years we were blessed with our daughter, Melissa, and son, Christian, both becoming the light and joy of our lives. Amidst the roles of parenting, I became a room mother, Fun Fair chairman, Girl Scout and PTA leader, as Dennis and I were honored throughout these years to serve in both school and church leadership.

The trials and triumphs of life at this juncture would be a book unto itself, and now that our children have children, the adventures of grandparenting yet another!

For taking the time to read my story, I offer sincere, heartfelt gratitude and pray it has been some source of encouragement to you on your journey. Whatever path life has taken or rocky places along the way, it is never too late for God's intervention, for He is the Redeemer of all and the Master of happy endings.

May God richly bless you.

LaVergne, TN USA
27 December 2010
210214LV00002B/17/P